**Collins English**

D0794753

Series editors: K R Cripwell

A library of graded readers for students of English as a second or foreign language, and for reluctant native readers. The books are graded in six levels of difficulty. Structure, vocabulary, idiom and sentence length are all controlled according to principles laid down in detail in *A Guide to Collins English Library*. A list of the books follows. Numbers after each title indicate the level at which the book is written: 1 has a basic vocabulary of 300 words and appropriate structures, 2 : 600 words, 3 : 1000 words, 4 : 1500 words, 5 : 2000 words and 6 : 2500 words.

*Inspector Holt and the Fur Van* John Tully 1
*Where is Bill Ojo?* John Tully 1
*Crocodile!* K R Cripwell 1
*Four Short Stories* Margery Morris 1
*The Story of Macbeth* from Shakespeare 1
*Fast Money* K R Cripwell 1
*It's a Trick!* Lewis Jones 1
*Taxi!* Jane Homeshaw 1
*Tin Lizzie* Jane Homeshaw 1
*Dead in the Morning* Jane Homeshaw 1
*Letters from the Dead* Jane Homeshaw 1
*The Pathfinders* Jane Homeshaw 1
*Cats in the Dark* John Tully 1
*Inspector Holt Gets His Man* John Tully 1
*Inspector Holt and the Chinese Necklace* John Tully 1
*The Bridge* John Tully 2
*Muhammad Ali: King of the Ring* John Tully 2
*The Magic Garden* K R Cripwell 2
*The Wrestler* K R Cripwell 2
*The Titanic is Sinking* K R Cripwell 2
*The Canterville Ghost* Oscar Wilde 2
*The Prince and the Poor Boy* Mark Twain 2
*Two Roman Stories* from Shakespeare 2
*Oliver Twist* Charles Dickens 2
*The Story of Madame Tussaud's* Lewis Jones 2
*Three Sherlock Holmes Adventures* Sir A Conan Doyle 2
*The Story of Scotland Yard* Lewis Jones 2
*Charles and Diana* Margery Morris 2
*The Charlie Chaplin Story* Jane Homeshaw 2
*A King's Love Story* K R Cripwell 2
*Dangerous Earth* Jane Homeshaw 2
*Five Ghost Stories* Viola Huggins 3
*Brainbox and Bull* Michael Kenyon 3
*Climb a Lonely Hill* Lilith Norman 3

Collins English Library Level 2

# A King's Love Story

## K.R. CRIPWELL

Collins ELT

© K R Cripwell 1984

1 2 3 4 5 6 7 8 9 10

Printed and published in Great Britain by
William Collins Sons and Co Ltd
Glasgow G4 0NB

First published in Collins English Library 1984

ISBN 00 370153 0

Cover photograph of St. Edward's Crown,
Crown Copyright.
Cover design by Dan Lim.
Text photographs:
*Pages 7* and *bottom 29* BBC Hulton Picture Library.
*Pages 13, 15* and *top 29* Camera Press Ltd.

## The Royal Family Tree

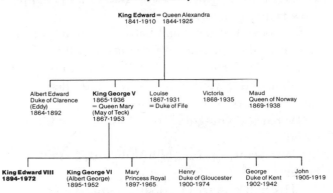

**King Edward** = Queen Alexandra
1841-1910    1844-1925

Albert Edward
Duke of Clarence
(Eddy)
1864-1892

**King George V**
1865-1936
= Queen Mary
(May of Teck)
1867-1953

Louise
1867-1931
= Duke of Fife

Victoria
1868-1935

Maud
Queen of Norway
1869-1938

**King Edward VIII**
**1894-1972**

**King George VI**
(Albert George)
1895-1952

Mary
Princess Royal
1897-1965

Henry
Duke of Gloucester
1900-1974

George
Duke of Kent
1902-1942

John
1905-1919

# Chapter 1
# Early Years

On 23rd June 1894 the Duke and Duchess of
York had a son. His great-grandmother was the
Queen of England – Queen Victoria.

People all over the world were happy for the
mother and father of the new prince. There were
letters from rich and poor people; from old and
young; from England, Wales, Scotland and
Ireland and from across the sea. Newspapers were
full of stories of the new prince and his family.

When Queen Victoria went to see her new

great-grandson, there were noisy and happy crowds along the roads.

She looked at the small baby with blue eyes in the arms of his mother. "One day you'll be King of England," she thought. "But you must wait for that. First your grandfather and then your father must be king before you."

"What are you going to call him?" the Queen asked.

"We want to call him Edward," said his father.

"His name must be Albert," said the Queen. "Albert was my dear husband's name, and all my sons and grandsons and great-grandsons must be called Albert. His name is Albert."

"But we want to call him Edward," said her grandson. "We want to call him Edward for my brother. He's dead but my son will carry his name."

"Your brother's name was Albert Victor," said the Queen. "Edward was just another name."

"Then we'll call him Edward Albert."

In the end, the baby's names were Edward Albert Christian George Andrew Patrick David. George was for England, Andrew for Scotland, Patrick for Ireland and David for Wales. But in the family his name was always David.

*Queen Victoria holding Edward the 8th, with Edward the 7th on the left, George the 5th on the right.*

6

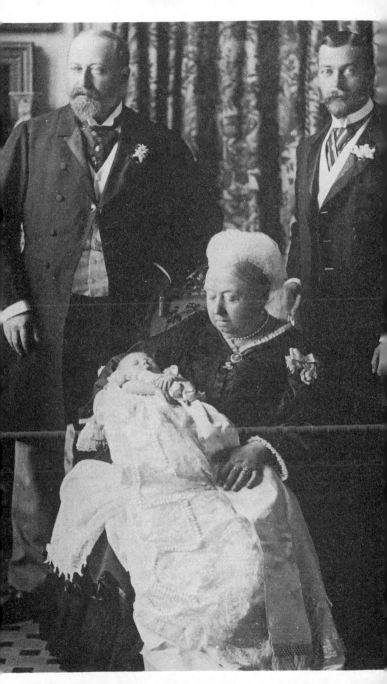

The family of the Duke of York lived like many other rich families of the time. They went out a lot. They visited the homes of friends, and others in the Royal family. During the winter there were dinners and dances. In the summer they went to the country, and in the autumn the men shot and fished. Every year was the same. There was little time for books or music. Sports and horses and guns and pretty dresses filled the time. But the world of adults was not the same for the children. Young children stayed at home. They saw their parents once or sometimes twice a day. These visits were short, and they wore their best clothes.

Edward was one year older than his brother Albert, and two years older than his sister, Alice. They lived together in two rooms of York Cottage. They all played and ate in one room, and slept in the other.

The Duke and Duchess didn't see their children often. They loved them but they didn't play with them. The Duke spoke to his children like one man to another in the army. They were afraid of him and his voice. The Duchess loved her children, but she didn't like to show her love for them in any way. When Prince Edward cried she said, "Take him away. He cries too much, and I don't like cry-babies." Many people said that she was a cold mother. Later, Prince Edward said, "There was little love in our house."

Soon it was time for Edward and Albert to start

their lessons with the Duchess's old teacher, Madame Bricka. But their school only had the children of the family in it. When Edward was nine he went to a dancing class. There were about 30 children, and his mother knew all of their mothers and fathers. But he and his brothers and sisters didn't often meet other children like this.

Then in 1904, when Prince Edward was 10 years old, his great-grandmother Queen Victoria died. There were lots of changes in his family's life. His grandfather was now the King of England – Edward the 7th. His father and his mother moved from the small home in York Cottage to Marlborough House in London, Frogmore House in Windsor, and Abergeldie Castle in Scotland. Edward was one step nearer to the King of England.

# Chapter 2
# A Man's World

The young princes never went to school. They had a teacher called Mr Hansell. But he was a better sportsman than a teacher. He tried his best, but his best was not very good. He put two desks, a blackboard and some books in one of the rooms in York Cottage. That was the classroom. From 7.30 to 8.15 before breakfast, and from 9 to 1, and between 5 and 6, they did their lessons. Sometimes there was a game of football with the boys from the village school. There were also teachers from outside for French and German. At Sandringham a teacher in the village school took them for walks in the country.

Once, when Prince Edward was 12 and his brother was 10, they were at Abergeldie Castle in Scotland. After a shoot, their father pointed to the dead animals. "How heavy are all these animals? I've written a number for each one in this book." The two boys tried hard, but each time they got a different answer. "What's wrong with you?" their father cried. "You need another teacher." So a teacher in the village school came to the castle every day, to teach the two young princes more about numbers.

The houses of the Royal Family were full of famous pictures. But no one told Edward and Albert about them. There were lots of Scottish music and army music, but no other music. Music and pictures were not for boys. Only girls talked about those things. Boys learned to shoot and fish and ride on horses. Their father taught the boys to shoot. But they were not good riders, and not very good at sport either.

When Prince Edward was 14, his father sent him into the Navy. His brother went with him. At that time, the Navy took boys of 13 or 14, and taught them some science. They also learned about ships. Edward and his brother Albert did not do very well. Their lessons with Mr Hansell were not enough, and often they were last in the class. There were often some unfriendly words when their father got letters from the Navy teachers about the two young princes.

Life at the Navy school was hard for the young Princes. They lived in a big room with thirty other boys. They got up at 6.30 in winter, cleaned their teeth, and then jumped into a cold bath for a swim. They ran all the time, and the food was often bad. Sunday afternoons were free.

The boys at the Navy school were like most boys. They asked questions about Edward and his family. Edward often did not want to answer, or couldn't, so the boys laughed at him. Edward was not afraid, but he made few friends. He was the same as other boys but different. Kings and the sons of Kings cannot have friends like other people.

Then his grandfather, King Edward the 7th, died. Edward's father was now King. Then on Edward's sixteenth birthday, he became the Prince of Wales. Then his father sent him to sea for three months.

After his four years at Navy schools, the Prince went to Oxford. He took Mr Hansell with him. He had very few young friends. All the time around him were old men – his Oxford teacher and Mr Hansell. He was not a very good learner, but in his second year he became part of Oxford life.

Then in August 1914, World War One started. The Prince went into the army. Later in the year he went to France. The army did not want to send him to the fighting. "You are the King's son," they said. The Prince answered, "But I have four brothers." He made a number of visits to the soldiers at war, and they liked him. People began to talk of the Prince of Wales. For the first time, people began to know the first son of the King. He visited the army in the middle east, in Italy, and France.

Then, after the war, he began to make visits all over the world. He was 25 when he went to Canada and the United States. There were crowds all the way. All the world wanted to see the young Prince of Wales. He was not very tall but he had bright blue eyes and a warm smile. Later he went to New Zealand and Australia, and then India and South Africa.

People wanted to forget the war and the times before the war. They wanted happy times, happy music, happy dances, happy things. They loved the new and the young. The Prince of Wales was happy and new and young. He was the man for the times.

But the Prince was a man's man. While he was

*The Prince of Wales visiting Scottish soldiers in France during World War One.*

growing up there were only men around him: Mr Hansell, his father, his teachers in the Navy and at Oxford, the army during the war. He had few friends of the same age. There were his brothers, the village boys who came to play football, the Navy boys. It was a world of men and boys. He knew very little about girls and women.

# Chapter 3
## Waiting

''Who's he going to marry?'' ''Who's going to be his wife?'' ''Will she be a princess?'' ''Will she be English or from another country?'' ''Is she rich?''

"What does she do now?" "Is she a filmstar?"

For every question there were hundreds of answers. People looked closely at every woman who talked or danced with the prince. Pictures in the newspapers often showed the prince with one woman or another – at a restaurant, a great house, at a party, at a new bridge or building or at a school, in any part of the world. People looked hard at each one and talked about her – until the next picture. Over the years, there were lots of them.

During the war, Prince Edward had a job. He was a soldier in the British army. But after the war he had no job. He could only wait for his job, because his father, King George the 5th, had his job. He was the King. When King George died, Edward could be King. His father became King of England in 1910. In 1919 the Prince of Wales came home from the war. He was 25 years old.

What did he do while he waited? Lots of things. He opened new buildings and roads. And he travelled to many other countries.

The 1920's and 1930's were not happy times. There was no work, and many people lost their jobs. There was no money for clothes or food or houses. Sick children stood on street corners with their hands out. "Please give me some money or some food," their eyes said. The Prince could not change the world. But he could see and tell others. People listened to him because he was the Prince of Wales. He told them about people without work. He talked about the sick children with little food. He asked for help. He worked hard to help his people. And the people loved him for it. Where the Prince went, there were always crowds of happy people.

But the Prince was also a young man. He loved two things very much. One was horses, and the other was parties. He rode hard, and he loved high jumps over walls and bushes. He liked to be in front of others, and often he came first. But this kind of riding is dangerous. One day, he had a bad fall. "David, you must stop," said his mother, Queen Mary. "It's too dangerous. Your father's ill and I need you now. Sell your horses and play some other sport." And he did.

*The Prince of Wales riding hard.*

But he did not stop his parties. He loved good talk and good food. He also liked dancing and dance music. Sometimes he had small parties for his close friends at Windsor. Often he went to parties in other people's houses, or in hotels and famous restaurants. Many parties ended in the early hours of the morning. He met many people at these parties, but very few men and women became his close friends.

The Prince fell in love first when he was 21. It was in the middle of World War One. He spent part of the summer at Sandringham. Lord Leicester's house was near Sandringham, and each family often visited the other. The Prince met Lady Coke there. She was the wife of Lord Leicester's son. The Prince fell in love with her. She was small and full of life. But she was 12 years older than him, and she also had a husband. While he was away in the army, he wrote long love letters to her. This love came to an end three years later.

In the spring of 1918, he spent six weeks in England. Some people say that he fell in love for a second time then. This time it was the daughter of the Duke of Sutherland, Lady Rosemary Leveson-Gower. Lady Cynthia Asquith wrote, ''He dances most with Rosemary, and drives with her in the day-time.'' But she was not a princess, and perhaps she didn't want to be the Queen of England. A year later she married a friend of the

Prince of Wales.

One evening in early March 1918, a young woman and a man walked through Belgrave Square in London. Her name was Freda Dudley Ward. She was married and she had two children. There was a party in one of the houses. Music and light came through the open front door. It was still wartime. Suddenly there was a loud noise. "German planes," cried the man. "We must hide. Let's go in here." They ran through the door into the house. Inside they met the people at the party. "Come on," they said. "Follow us, down the stairs to the lower floor."

In the dark, Mrs Dudley Ward stood next to a young man.

"Where do you live?" he asked.

"With my husband's mother," she said. "Where do you live?"

"In London sometimes, and sometimes at Windsor," he answered.

They talked like this for some time. The German planes went away and the people went upstairs. Freda Ward and her friend wanted to leave, but a woman in a long green dress said, "Don't go. This is my house. It's my party, and the Prince of Wales wants you to stay."

Freda went upstairs and danced with the Prince of Wales all night. After the party, he took her home in his car. The next day he called on her.

For the next 16 years, the Prince and Mrs Freda Dudley Ward were very close friends. He was in love with her, but he couldn't marry her.

A few people knew about the Prince's love, because they saw him with her all the time. The newspapers said nothing. Sometimes there was a picture of the Prince with her, but she was just another woman in a long line of them. So most people didn't know about it.

But it was love. Every day, when he could, the Prince visited her at 5 o'clock in her London home. Sometimes he stayed for dinner, and sometimes they went out to dinner together. During the summers, he had a house next to her house at Sandwich. They visited other people's houses together. Where she went, he followed. Like him, she was small and full of life. She was pretty, with light hair and bright eyes. She called him 'The Little Prince'.

The King and the Queen were not happy about this. "Why can't he fall in love with a girl without a husband? What does he see in her? He can never marry her. She can never be his wife or the Queen." The King tried to talk to his son about Mrs Dudley Ward. He spoke like a father to a young boy. But the Prince was not a young boy – he was nearly 40 years old now. He closed his ears and did not listen. His love for Freda was too strong.

Then he met Wallis Simpson.

# Chapter 4
## Wallis Warfield Simpson

Wallis came from America, and she was two years younger than the Prince of Wales. Both her mother and father came from old American families. Her real first name was Bessiewallis – Wallis after her father's name, and Bessie after her aunt's name. She didn't like the name Bessie. "It's a cow's name," she said. So she changed it to Wallis.

Her father died when she was five months old. After that, she and her mother lived with her father's family. Her mother's family was a rich one. They still had town houses, and farms in the country. Her father's family were rich once, but no more. For some time she and her mother had hard times, but her Aunt Bessie often helped. Her mother married again.

In 1916 Wallis marrried Earl Winfield Spencer. He was a flier in the US Navy. He had good looks but not very much money. He was not a very good husband. Wallis liked parties, but Win didn't like it when she talked and laughed with other men. He began to drink too much. One day he put her in the bathroom and wouldn't let her out for hours. The next day she went to her mother.

"I can't live with Win," she said. "I don't want to be his wife any more. I must get a divorce."

"You can't have a divorce, Wallis," said her mother, "can she, Aunt Bessie?"

"No. No divorce in our family."

"What can I do?" asked Wallis.

"Talk to him. Perhaps you can live in different places for a time," answered Aunt Bessie. "Then start again."

"But no divorce, Wallis," said her mother.

Wallis talked to her husband. "I'm sorry, Wallis," he said, "I can't help you. I'm going to China. You stay here in Washington. If you want me, I'll be back."

Win and Wallis met once more in China but there was no change. "I must have my divorce, Win," Wallis said. He stayed, and she went back to America. She asked about divorces. "If you and your husband do not live together for three years, you can get a divorce. But you must spend one year in Virginia after you start the divorce." In December 1927 the marriage with Win was over. She had her divorce.

Wallis met Ernest Simpson and his wife in New York, before her divorce from Win. He was the son of an English father and an American mother. He came from New York. He was not happy with his wife, and soon he divorced her. Then he

20

moved to work in London. Wallis followed, and in the summer of 1928 she and Ernest were married. She was now Mrs Wallis Warfield Simpson and Ernest was her second husband.

Ernest Simpson's family was a rich one, and soon Wallis met many rich and famous people in London. They were the same people who met the Prince of Wales. In 1930, when she was 36 years old, Wallis Simpson met the Prince of Wales. She saw him again six months later. They began to meet more and more. Then in January 1932 he asked her to come to Fort Belvedere, his home near Windsor Castle. She came with her husband and some other people. She came more and more often.

The Prince forgot Mrs Dudley Ward. He was in love with Mrs Simpson.

Mrs Simpson began to see less and less of her husband. He went to the USA on business, while she went with the Prince and his friends to the south of France. Aunt Bessie went with her. They went by boat to Italy. People could see the love of each for the other. Back in England, she met the King and Queen for the first and last time, when Prince Albert got married. The King's family was cold towards her. Only Lord Mountbatten, the Prince's uncle, visited Fort Belvedere now.

The King was old and sick. He spoke to his son about his clothes, but he never spoke about Mrs Simpson. But Edward's father and mother never talked about things like love to their children. The Prince was in love with Mrs Simpson, and he wanted to marry her. He didn't talk to his father or the family about it. All his life, he got things when he wanted them. He was the Prince of Wales.

On Monday 20 January 1936, King George the 5th died at Sandringham, with his family around his bed. His wife, Queen Mary, took the hand of her oldest son and said, "The King is dead. Now you are King."

The Prince of Wales became King Edward the 8th.

# Chapter 5
# The Divorce

Wallis Simpson stood at a window with the new King, and the next day there was a picture of her and the new King in the newspapers. But the newspapers didn't give her name.

Edward began his work as King, but he didn't forget Mrs Simpson. Then in the summer he went on holiday. This time he went by train to Yugoslavia. There he took a boat to the Greek islands and on to Istanbul. He took a few friends and Mrs

Simpson. There were crowds at every stop. People wanted to see the new King. But they also wanted to see Mrs Simpson. In England the newspapers said nothing about Mrs Simpson, but in other countries the newspapers were full of stories about her and the King. There were photographs of the King and Mrs Simpson together in a car, on the sand, by the sea. In a small boat, her hand on his arm, his eyes on her face. Most of the world outside England knew about her.

Back in England he told his mother, "I'm going to go to Balmoral in Scotland, for the last two weeks of September."

"I'm so glad, David," she said. "We all love Balmoral best of our homes. It's a real family home." But he hurt his mother. He asked Mrs Simpson too.

The King still wanted to marry Wallis. But she was still married to Ernest Simpson. The only way was a divorce.

"I'm in love with the King," Wallis said to her husband.

"I know. What are you going to do about it?"

"I must have a divorce."

"I can't divorce you, Wallis. I can't say that the King is your lover."

"I know. Then I must divorce you."

"All right."

A few weeks later, Ernest Simpson gave Wallis

some pictures. They showed him and a woman in a hotel bedroom together. "Now you can divorce me because of another woman," he said. "But it will take a year for the divorce."

The King spoke to the newspapers. "Please don't write about this divorce," he said. "It will hurt Mrs Simpson. Don't hurt her just because she is the friend of the King." The newspapers said nothing about the divorce.

But the newspapers in other countries didn't keep quiet. The news of the King's love was hot. Letters started to come to Buckingham Palace. There were letters to the Queen Mother, Queen Mary. Many people said that the King must not marry Mrs Simpson.

The Archbishop of Canterbury spoke to the King. "You can't marry Mrs Simpson," he said. "You are the head of the Church of England. But in our church a woman who is divorced can't marry again. Mrs Simpson is divorced, with a second husband. You can't marry her in my church."

The head of the Government was Stanley Baldwin, and he also spoke to the King.

"You're young. You like children. But you're not married. Your country wants you to marry. We all want you to marry and have children. We want a Queen. But this business with Mrs Simpson is no good. Let her go. Stop the divorce."

"I can't," said the King. "She's the only woman in the world for me, and I can't live without her."

"There's going to be lots of talk," said Baldwin.

"Let them talk," said the King. And there was talk. In Canada and Australia, stories about the King and Mrs Simpson passed from mouth to mouth. Many were not true, but some people believed them. "What's that woman doing to the King? We don't want her to be Queen of England," people said.

Then in October, Wallis got the first part of her divorce. "In six months I'll be free. I can marry again," she said.

The Government didn't want the marriage. "He can marry Mrs Simpson. But if he does marry her, this Government goes. He knows this. It's the King or the Government." Baldwin went to Buckingham Palace to talk to the King again.

"The wife of the King of England is different from other wives," Baldwin said to the King. "The wife of the King becomes this country's Queen. And so you must listen to the voice of the people. The people will not have Mrs Simpson for their Queen."

"All right. I won't be King. My brother can be King. And I'll marry Mrs Simpson."

"I'm very sorry to hear that," answered Baldwin.

"I'll tell my mother about this tonight."

After dinner that night he sat with his mother and his sister, Mary.

"I'm going to marry Wallis," he said.

"You can't David," said his mother. "She's divorced. You can't marry her. The church won't let you."

"I must, mother. I love her."

"The people will not have her, David."

"Then I must go."

"You mean – the country will lose you?"

"Yes, Mary. If that is the price."

"You never think of others. It's always only I, I, I. Isn't it?"

"We're in love, isn't that enough?"

"No it isn't, for a King of England. I don't want to meet her. Who will take your place? Have you thought of that?"

"Bertie. He'll be a much better King than me."

"Does he know?"

"Not yet."

"Always take the easy way, don't you. Did you think about your brother? Just give him the job because you're too small for it."

There was one other way.

"Perhaps Mrs Simpson can be your wife, but not the Queen of England," said a friend to the King. "If you have children, they won't be princes and princesses. The next King will then be your brother, Albert. And after him, his children.''

In the end, Baldwin asked Britain's friends in the governments of other countries three questions:

1   Can Mrs Simpson marry the King and become Queen?
2   Can Mrs Simpson marry the King and not become Queen?
3   Must the King go?

The answers were No, No and Yes. The King must go.


# Chapter 6
# The Last Days


On 3 December, Mrs Simpson left England for France. And four days later the King told Baldwin, ''I will leave soon.''

It was time for goodbyes. He had a dinner at Fort Belvedere with his brothers and a few close friends, and Baldwin. No women. The King was happy, with a smile on his face. All the others had sad faces. Then there was a visit to see his mother. The Queen Mother said, ''David, you're losing all this for one woman!'' Later he put his name on the papers and sent them to the Government. He was the King no more.

Then he asked to speak on the radio. He wanted to tell the people why he had to go. After a last dinner with his family, a car took him to Windsor Castle.

"This is Windsor Castle . . ."

The Prince began to speak.

"It's time for me to say a few words to you." He talked about his country, as the Prince of Wales and later as King. He talked about the new King, his brother.

"I cannot go on without the help of the woman I love," he said. "And now we all have a new King. I hope with all my heart that happiness will be his – and yours."

# Chapter 7
## The End of the Story

King Edward the 8th now became Prince Edward, the Duke of Windsor. He married Wallis in the south of France on 3 June 1937. He was 43 and she was 41. Wallis, now the Duchess

Top: *The Duke and Duchess of Windsor on their wedding day.*
Bottom: *The wedding day – many homes in London had signs like this one.*

of Windsor, wore a long blue dress and coat, and a blue hat. Now, after all this time, she was Edward's wife.

The Duke visited England when his brother, King George the 6th, died, and again when his mother died. But he went alone.

He died in May 1972.

He lost a country, and won a woman's love.

LONG LIFE & HAPPINESS TO THE DUKE OF WINDSOR

A KING SHALL REIGN — A KING SHALL FALL
IT MEANS BUT LITTLE — LOVE MEANS ALL

# A Word Game

Here's a crossword for you. All the answers come from this book.

Good luck!

## Across

1 Edward became the _____ of Windsor.
4 Edward _____ his name on the papers, and he was king no more.
7 Young Edward was the same _____ other boys, but different.
9 Edward loved to ride one.
11 Edward's great-grandmother.
12 Friendly governments' answer to the question: "Can Mrs Simpson marry the King and not become Queen?"
16 Mr Hansell gave lessons in a room at York _____.
18 When the young prince tried to work with numbers, he got a different answer _____ time.
19 In the Prince of Wales' family, _____ was called David.
20 Edward often went to these, in hotels and people's homes.
21 In World War One, Edward went into the _____.
22 Edward not was Wallis's first husband, but the _____.

## Down

1 Wallis _____ her second husband.
2 The boys in the royal family learned to fish and _____.

3    The name Andrew was _____ Scotland.

4    At 16, Edward became the _____ of Wales.

5    Wallis Simpson came from this country.

6    Edward's father was _____ George.

8    1914 was the _____ of World War One.

10   Who fell in love with Freda Ward?

13   The Prince of Wales became King Edward the _____.

14   Queen Mary was Edward's _____.

15   When Queen Victoria died, Edward was one _____ nearer to the King.

17   In 1927, Wallis's first marriage was _____.

## Answers

**Down**

1 divorced 2 shoot 3 for 4 Prince 5 USA 6 King 8 start 10 Edward 13 eighth 14 mother 15 step 17 over

**Across**

1 Duke 4 put 7 as 9 horse 11 Victoria 12 no 16 Cottage 18 every 19 he 20 parties 21 army 22 third